The White Cliffs of Dover

Images of Cliff and Shore

by Peter and Julie Burville

Published by
Triangle Publications, Dover
© Peter and Julie Burville

ISBN 0-9539478-1-5

Typeset in Plantin Light
by Dr. and Mrs P. J. Burville

Printed in Great Britain by
A.R. Adams & Sons (Printers) Ltd
Dover

Front Cover illustration:
Dover's Eastern Cliffs c1891, a photograph from the Dover Museum collection.

Contents and Image Sequence

★ Images 4, 13, 14, 18, 19, 20 and 41 are reproduced in colour in the centre pages.

Acknowledgements

With grateful thanks to the Dover Museum, in particular Christine Waterman, Jon Iveson, Mark Frost and Margaret Sharp, also to Trefor Baylis for his drawing used in the Introduction, but especially to Liz Owen and Bryan Williams for their patience and expertise so generously given over the past four years.

Further thanks to:

The Public Record Office, Kew for permission to publish part of the Guston tithe map (Image 16);

Dover Public Library for permission to use Images 1, 2, 20, 22, 24, 25, 32, 33, 34 and 37;

Bob Hollingsbee for the loan of the original photographic plates for Images 21, 28 and 36;

Dover Harbour Board for providing Images 39, 40 and 41;

Dover Museum for all the other Images;

Merril Lilley, of the Dover Society, for her assistance in the later stages of this project.

Finally, we would like to thank Dover Harbour Board for their generous sponsorship for the production of this book.

Foreword

This book arises from research carried out by the authors as volunteer workers at Dover Museum. The original project was to provide a commentary for some of the many images on the Museum's collection public-access database.

The authors chose to concentrate on images of the East Cliff area of Dover. From the wealth of material available, it soon became apparent that a pictorial history of this locale would make an interesting book.

The final selection of images for this publication spans four centuries and records change and development up to the present day. The collection provides glimpses into a fascinating environment, its habitations, inhabitants and their ways of earning a living, now long gone.

Some of the images and information have previously featured in *The Dover Society Newsletter*.

Introduction

The white cliffs of Dover, a symbol of England world-wide, are made of chalk, a soft limestone, studded with horizontal bands of flint. Chalk was formed from the sedimentary remains of planktonic algae and other marine debris such as the shells of molluscs. It has been suggested that minute algae suspended in sea-water would have been eaten by small shrimps and passed out as heavier faeces which then sank, as proto-chalk, to the seabed.

The flint was formed from the remains of innumerable sponges that settled into horizontal layers within the forming chalk. When washed from the chalk and pounded by the waves, the flints create our local beach shingle.

The process of chalk formation, (at a rate of about 1 inch per 1,000 years), took place during the Upper Cretaceous period that lasted from 100 million to 70 million years ago. These deposits have provided both materials for men to work with and fossils to catalogue the past.

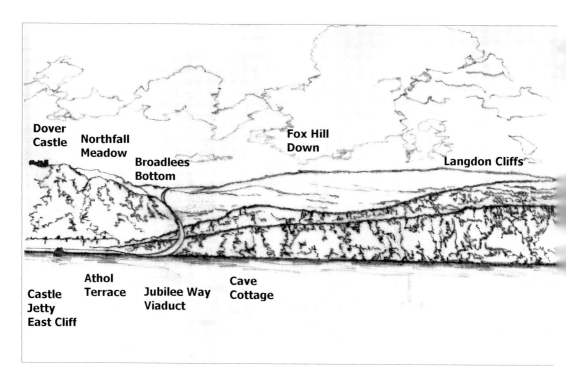

This diagrammatic representation of today's cliffs provides the reader with a locative framework for the commentaries associated with the historic images. The term 'Hole', as in Langdon Hole and Fan Hole, is a contraction of 'hollow'.

Flint has served man throughout the ages. It supplied one of the major tool materials of the Stone Age and, more recently, the spark for flintlock firearms. Today, a related silicone form provides raw material for computer-chips. Chalk has also contributed to Information Technology, having been used on slate and blackboard by generations of schoolchildren and their teachers. Over the millennia, chalk has been used both as a basic building material and as a source for lime.

Man, as well as nature, has sculptured Dover's famous white walls. At the end of the 19th century, the construction of the Admiralty or National Harbour necessitated the cutting back and facing of hundreds of yards of Dover's eastern cliffs. This realignment modified the natural cliff outline and obliterated the evidence of a recent troglodyte (cave dwelling) culture. Fortunately, all is not lost. Paintings, sketches, engravings and early photographs from Dover collections provide a fascinating record of the changing cliffs through time.

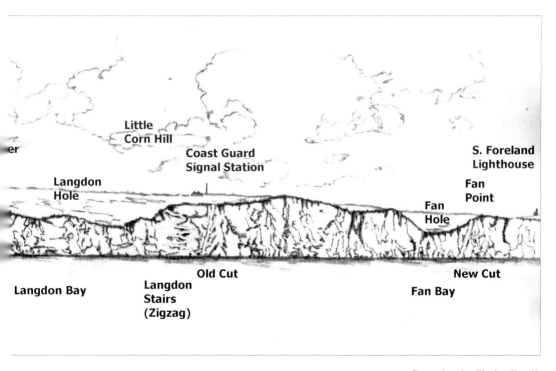

Drawing by Trefor Baylis

Part one:
The East Cliff Area

Two drawings by E. Bradley provide an economical but accurate panorama of the chalk cliffs east of Dover. The artist captures the dominance of the towering cliffs and the remoteness of the East Cliff, Athol Terrace, Guston Cliff area.

Image 1: Bradley's view "East Cliffs, Dover" September 2nd 1876

This eastward-looking view, sketched from the sea, shows, from left to right: Broadlees Bottom, Northfall Meadow, Fox Hill Down, Langdon Cliff, The Cobbler (or Cobbler Point), Langdon Hole, Corn Hill with its Coast Guard station, Fan Hole, Fan Point, and the South Foreland towards St Margaret's Bay.

Part-way up the cliff face, and meandering over the remnants of chalk falls, are paths associated with the entrances of several caves. The most prominent dark hole on the widest stretch of path is almost certainly the tunnel, excavated in 1870, to link East Cliff with the cliff-top (see Image 28a).

Some of the caves were used for storage, such as the twin caves below the path and to the left of the picture. Others, not depicted in this drawing, were used for human habitation in the 19th century (see Images 13, 14, 16 and 21f).

The lines on the cliff-top represent fencing erected on land at Broadlees Bottom owned by the Earl of Guilford. The vertical line on the sea side of the enclosure is probably the Earl's notice board (see Image 25).

To the east, on Cornhill, is the coastguard signalling station or signal house. Below, cut into the cliff-face, is the zigzag path, sometimes known as Langdon Stairs. This path gave the coastguards access to their cutters on the beach below. The rowing boat, manned by three pairs of oars is likely to be a coastguard cutter or possibly a pilot-boat waiting to guide larger shipping into harbour.

The cut, the vertical channel down the face of the cliff east of the zigzag, was used to raise material from the shore. Items hauled from the beach would have included fresh water from the chalk springs, seaweed to fertilise the land, flints and even useful flotsam and jetsam and, later, essential supplies to the remote Coastguard station.

In "Rambling Recollections of the Neighbourhood of Dover" (1848), William Burgess writes:

> *'Below this* (the Coastguard Station) *there is an easy descent to the beach - a zigzag in the cliff, named Langdon Stairs - at the end of this a windlass was used to draw heavy articles from the beach, and not only heavy articles but such light goods, as they were termed by the Free-traders* (smugglers) *who flourished before the days of the Coast Blockade.'*

Bradley has sketched various sailing and rowing craft, and what appears to be a mooring-buoy floating in the foreground.

Image 2: Bradley's view "East Cliff & Athol Terrace" March 29th 1877

The westward view of East Cliff and Athol Terrace is sketched from the beach. It looks towards Castle (East Cliff) Jetty, Sydney Villa and Athol Terrace, with Shakespeare Cliff in the background. The latter is so named because of the numerous references to the cliff in Shakespeare's "King Lear". The blinded Gloucester talks of a cliff at Dover *'whose high and bending head/ Looks fearfully in the confined deep.'* Edgar, Gloucester's son, conjures the place more vividly:

'*... half-way down | Hangs one that gathers samphire, dreadful trade!| Methinks he seems no bigger than his head. | The fishermen that walk upon the beach | Appear like mice, and yond tall anchoring bark | Diminish'd to her cock, her cock a buoy | Almost too small to sight ...'*

The foreground figure, in the sketch, carries circular prawning nets in his left hand. Draped down his back are the cork floats of his nets. He shoulders a forked pole used to place and retrieve his nets from the rock pools and gullies. This drop-net method continues to be used by the authors and other local prawners today.

Between the prawner and a second, seated figure, a steep pathway, or steps, leads to the higher level track where a cave entrance is visible.

On one side of the seated figure is a fork, or spade, on the other a large basket suggesting that he may have been collecting seaweed, a useful marine harvest to help fertilise the land. The seaweed would have been carried into Dover by cart, or hauled up the old cut in the cliffs at Langdon Hole. This, and a similar cut made later to the east in the Fan Hole cliff, are still very much in evidence today.

A small craft is being rowed close to the shore. There is no evidence of capstans or such to indicate an established landing place on this stretch of beach.

Image 3: "Jetty Cliffs Dover" circa 1835

This sketch, by an unknown artist, shows a higher and lower path. The former is a section of the path viewed from the sea in the eastward-looking Bradley sketch.

There are several walkers. One of the two foreground figures carries a long staff, or pole, over his shoulder. His hat has a somewhat military appearance, in which case the staff might be a pike and the uniform that of a counter-smuggling or blockade officer on his way to the watch house and signalling station on the cliff-top at Corn Hill. Alternatively, the staff could be a prawning-pole, used to retrieve drop-nets from the sea.

At the end of the path is a construction that is apparently an extension to a cave. The higher path is fenced at the furthest bend, a security feature suggesting that horse-drawn carts use the route.

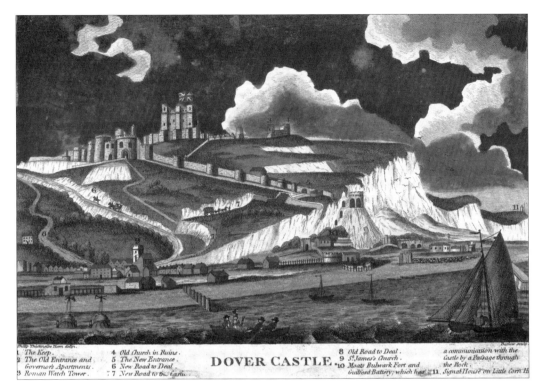

1. The Keep.
2. The Old Entrance and Governors Apartments.
3. Roman Watch Tower.
4. Old Church in Ruins.
5. The New Entrance.
6. New Road to Deal.
7. New Road to the Castle.

DOVER CASTLE

8. Old Road to Deal.
9. St James's Church.
10. Moats Bulwark Fort and Guilford Battery; which has

a communication with the Castle by a Passage through the Rock.
11. Signal House on Little Corn Hill

Image 4: Dover Castle circa 1810
(This image is reproduced in colour in the centre pages).

This annotated and charming coloured engraving shows features of Dover extending from the old Deal Road to the Signal House on Little Corn Hill at the eastern extremity. The engraving provides a good view of the early development at East Cliff. Behind a sea wall, and beneath the towering castle cliff with its associated chalk falls, are the complex of grottoes, castellated towers and boat-shaped roofs known as Smith's Folly.

Part two:
Smith's Folly and Grotto

Smith's Folly, the Grotto and buildings to the west are clearly shown in John Rennie's Plan of the Town and Harbour of Dover, dated 1805.

Image 5: "The Marine Villa of John Smith Esq."

Based on a drawing by John Nixon, this early engraving of 1801 depicts the unlikely under-cliff construction of Gothic walls, towers and castellation built in 1791 by John Smith and known as Smith's Folly. John Spencer Smith was an Army captain and aide-de-camp to Lord Sackville at the battle of Minden, Germany in August 1759. John's son was the Admiral Sir Sydney Smith GCB who had greater claim to fame.

In 1808 Edward Wedlake Brayley wrote of Smith's Folly, describing it as being constructed of flints and chalk. The folly consisted of various low buildings around a small courtyard, so that its general aspect resembled a fort. Projecting from the Folly's square tower on the seaward side was a wooden balcony supported by sturdy legs. In the middle of the complex, a flagpole topped the spire.

Large inverted boats, pitched with tar, provided roofs for the single storey buildings. These roofs are believed to be the inspiration for the similar beach dwelling described by Charles Dickens in "David Copperfield".

On the extreme left are some ecclesiastical looking buildings, with Gothic arched windows, associated with a series of caves known as the Grotto. Strollers in the foreground would seem to be admiring this eccentric architecture. From their appearance, the roofed buildings look in disrepair. Part of this cave complex still exists, and is in private ownership. Appended to the cliff above the Grotto is a series of dovecotes.

There is no sign of a sea wall; the only obvious sea-defence being an haphazard line of piled rocks running from behind the clinker-built boat to the folly.

Other features of interest are:

   i) Castle Jetty (begun in 1752) that projects into the sea to the east of the folly.

  ii) the two rows of portable crossed-barriers known as Cheval/Chevaux de Frise (translated as horse/horses of Friesland from the area where they were first deployed). The construction of a Cheval de Frise was normally a large joist, with six sides, from which projected iron-pointed spikes about six feet long and crossing one another. Their military use was to check cavalry charges and the like.

 iii) the zigzag path that climbs the cliff-fall at the rear of the Folly probably gave access to a higher level cave, though by 1825 there was a cottage built on this site.

Image 6: Engraving by G.B. Campion, 1824

This engraving, inaccurately titled "View from Smith's Folly", shows the Folly, the wooden construction of Castle Jetty, the harbour entrance, distant buildings on the Western Heights and the peak of Shakespeare Cliff just visible above the heights.

At this date the inland tower of the Folly has lost the tip of its spire, presumably the casualty of some winter storm, and is now topped with a weather vane. In this engraving the castellated towers, previously depicted as linear, are made to look picturesquely round. Further artistic licence seems to have been taken with the grand sea-front houses shown to the left of Smith's Folly. The houses on the Esplanade at the western horn of the bay were not commenced until 1833, nine years after the date of this engraving. Those depicted are probably the newly built Marine Parade, completed in 1820 (part of which, Marine Court, was demolished in 2000), though they were unlikely to be seen from this viewing point.

Hugging the cliff, where the Georgian Athol Terrace now stands, are simple, mainly single storey, cottages. These dwellings and their roadway are built on the platform created by an old cliff-fall.

The figure emerging from the cottage in the foreground appears to be loading goods into the horse-drawn cart. An undercliff residence might seem an unlikely location for a carrier, but 19th century census records confirm the carrier-occupation for one of the residents. His legitimate cargoes would have included flint for cobblestones and building material, seaweed for fertiliser, and even barrels of the sweet, fresh water collected from springs in the low-tide chalk. What else he might have carried to supplement a meagre income, in hard times, may be left to fertile imaginations.

The top-hatted and seated figure in the foreground would appear to be a self-portrait of the artist and engraver, G.B. Campion.

Image 7: Water Colour of Smith's Folly, 1825

This painting, by an unknown artist, depicts the marine villa complex and Castle Jetty viewed from a westerly perspective. The spire has been given a more squat appearance though it still sports its flagpole. The nondescript building at the foot of the cliff is likely to be part of the complex associated with the Grotto. Perched on the top of a cliff-fall at the rear of the folly is a cottage with pitched roof. A wall forms a sweeping curve to make an enclosure in which there appear to be cattle at rest.

Image 8: Smith's Folly from the Jetty, 1825

This watercolour, by the same unknown artist, views Smith's Folly from the planked and walled Castle Jetty. The painting shows twin, castellated square towers with a wooden balcony at first floor level. The left-hand building of the complex has a boat-shaped roof, three arched doorways but no windows. On the right and to the rear is a Gothic-style arched gatehouse.

The folly site is dominated by both the grandeur of the towering white cliffs and a massive cliff-fall, dark with vegetation. The well-established cover of vegetation suggests the cliff-fall is of considerable age. This fall appears virtually unchanged today and can best be viewed from the bottom of Jubilee Way.

The following two sketches by the topographical draughtsman John Claude Nattes, 1765? - 1822, provide a detailed record of the entrances to the Grotto caves, built into the base of the cliff on the Dover side of Smith's Folly. The Grotto was built to accommodate John Smith's sarcophagus but, at his death, he was given a more conventional burial.

Image 9: "The Grotto in Dover Cliffs"

J.C.Nattes depicts three separate structures of ecclesiastical appearance that front the Grotto caves. Above the middle structure, with its open door, is what appears to be a number of dovecotes. Other intriguing structures are shown appended to the cliff-face. Could the lower unit of out-size pigeon-holes be intended as an encouragement to nesting gulls? The twin projections above the open door look like the top of a ladder, presumably positioned to give access to the man-made nesting site. Many people, including the authors, consider gulls' eggs a gourmet treat.

On the left, Cheval de Frise barriers have been recycled to become boundary fencing and chalk-cut steps lead up to the elaborate, two-storey structure. The latter is shown in more detail in the following sketch.

Image 10: "The Grotto in Dover Cliffs"

Nattes depicts a two-storey structure with a very church-like facade and what appears to be a bell-tower. It is built on a cliff-fall several feet above the other entrances to the Grotto and is reached by way of a long and curving flight of chalk-cut steps. This structure is divided from the lower Grotto entrances by a gate and Cheval de Frise fencing. The abundant shrub-type vegetation on the site is evidence of a planted garden.

At the foot of the steps is a bench and nearby a hand-pump indicating the availability of fresh water. An East Cliff cottage, built on the spot where the artist must have been sitting, was named Fountain Cottage. This 1841 property still exists today.

On the left of the picture are structures associated with Mote's Bulwark or Guilford Battery.

Part three:
Early Athol Terrace

Violent forces of nature were largely responsible for the pattern of settlement that became Athol Terrace and East Cliff.

Image 11: "Dover Cliffs from near Smith's Folly" circa 1824

Artist and engraver G.B. Campion looks east from Castle Jetty to the South Foreland. The view includes Broadlees Hole, Langdon Hole and Fan Hole. The cliff top construction between the latter two is a signalling station, located, not on Cobbler Point as it appears to be in this engraving, but on Corn Hill (sometimes referred to as Little Corn Hill). Corn Hill is still planted with grain crops to this day. Despite almost two centuries of ploughing, post-harvest visitors to the crown of Corn Hill may still find a shaft of about 18 inches square and over a yard deep. As this shaft precisely matches the location given on early maps, it may well be the original step of the old signalling station mast. Field walking reveals much brick debris around this spot. Whether this is evidence of the blockade station or more recent wartime building is a matter for conjecture.

The engraving depicts cottages on what is now the site of Athol Terrace. The under-cliff road is well defined. The carrier's horse and cart are again in evidence, in this view being driven in an easterly direction. At the back of the under-cliff road are at least five eroded cliff falls. The ones is the foreground are topped with vegetation, but there is no obvious sign of caves at any level. Access from road level to shore is by way of a steep path and a distant set of steps, while in the foreground a man carrying a woven fish-basket is apparently climbing onto the jetty by means of a ladder. People are promenading along both the unfenced jetty and the under-cliff road.

Although there is no evidence of permanent mooring facilities, two boats, one with a mast, are pulled up onto the beach at the surf's edge. One of the figures on the beach is shouldering an oar.

At sea, the channel is busy with shipping. The single masted vessels in the foreground, being followed by gulls, are likely to be fishing boats. The vessels in the distance are two-masters, plying their trade.

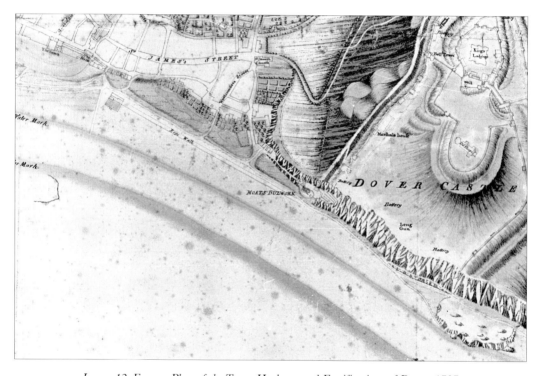

Image 12: From a Plan of the Town, Harbour and Fortifications of Dover, 1737

Early eighteenth century plans of Dover reveal a substantial, semi-circular platform at the base of the castle cliffs. This platform does not appear in earlier plans of Dover drawn in the reign of Henry VIII. The absence of such a substantial feature suggests it was created by a later massive cliff-fall, possibly caused by an earthquake. Such an event was recorded on 6th April 1580 when some cliff collapsed and Dover Castle lost part of its eastern wall. Indeed, another plan of Dover, printed c.1816, refers to this platform as New Head. However the 1816 plan does not show the 18th century Castle Jetty at East Cliff and was probably cribbed from a much earlier plan when the New Head would indeed have been new.

The original Athol Terrace properties were built on this extensive chalk platform. The platform resulted in the build-up of a shingle bank to the west, providing the necessary protection for the development of the East Cliff area for habitation.

With the erosion of the platform, the beach would have washed away and its loss may well have been the motivation for building the Castle Jetty at East Cliff. In "The History of Dover Harbour" by Alec Hasenson (1980), it states:

'... in 1752 Castle Jetty was begun, the latest of several groins (sic) *intended to help beach to accumulate against the shingle bank lying to the outer side of the Pent, thereby affording the latter greater protection against damage during storms.'*

The jetty and shingle bank it helped create would also have afforded protection to the military installations, such as the Mote's Bulwark at the foot of Castle Cliff. Also, in constructing his villa, subsequently known as Smith's Folly, John Smith would have had some confidence that his residence would be safe from the fearsome attack of storm-driven waves.

The plan shows two trackways, and a path at a higher level over a cliff-fall, in the East Cliff area. Whilst one track appears to terminate at the end of the chalk platform, the other goes along under the cliff towards St Margaret's Bay. These tracks gave access to caves in the cliffs, at this time an area designated as being in the parish of Guston. A century later the 1841 census return records that these caves had become permanent home for the family of carrier James Hart and for widow Mary Burville and her four children, whose late husband Benjamin was also a carrier.

Part four:
East Cliff Troglodytes

W.H. Prior, painted during the period 1833 -1857, when the term East Cliff was used to refer to the stretch of cliffs under Dover Castle and those in Dover's neighbouring parish of Guston. In his exterior and interior views of an East Cliff Cave-Cottage, Prior gives us an insight into the domestic arrangements of Dover's cave dwellers.

Image 13: "East Cliff Cave-Cottage"
(This image is reproduced in colour in the centre pages).

Prior's external view of the cave-cottage shows a chimney, three windows and a cleanly cut rectangular door. On the right, steps lead upward, perhaps to another cave (but see final paragraph below). Boundary walls, that appear to be made of cut chalk blocks rather than flint, create two enclosures. Oral history speaks of pigs being kept in caves in the cliffs. Could this be the explanation for these enclosures? East Cliff lore, passed down through the generations, also tells of the spoils of smuggling being wrapped in oilskin and hidden in barrels of pig manure for transportation under the olfactory-challenged noses of the excise men.

A track runs past the walls that separate the cave-cottage from an open, level area. In the foreground are several items of interest. The two square objects with their sloped appendages are most likely to be washboards and tubs. The Tithe map of Guston, Image 16, establishes this cave to be the cottage of a Burville family, while the Tithe return for 1843, and information for Guston in the 1851 Census, give the occupations of two of the cave-dwellers as 'Laundress'. These washerwomen were Mary Burville, a widow, and her daughter Elizabeth. The wooden bench on the right would have provided a welcome relief from the bending of their labours.

The six irregularly shaped objects resemble Roman-style anchors. They may have been the seabed trophies of Mary Burville's sons, Benjamin and William, both boatmen, who were living with her in the cave-cottage at the time of the 1851 census.

An account in the Dover Telegraph, dated 16th November 1833, records the premature death of carrier Benjamin Burville 'who, with his wife and several children, resided in a cave beneath the Castle Cliff.' Evidence of this cave and its occupant(s) exists in the 1850 photograph at Image 21f. The photograph, with a few exceptions, confirms the configuration of the cave's exterior detail as shown by Prior. Where the detail differs (e.g. the steps to the right of the cottage), it seems reasonable to assume this can be accounted for by artistic licence. Evidence that Prior took such liberties can be found in another of his watercolours, of the South Foreland, where the South Foreland lighthouse is shown on the skyline above Langdon Hole. Similar steps to those drawn by Prior could have been seen nearby, as in Wyndham's East Cliff Dover of 1869 (see Image 26).

The caves shown on the tithe map, and the cave entrances captured in this photograph, are firm locative evidence that Mary Burville's cave was situated below Northfall Meadow on top of a cliff-fall.

Image 14: "Cave-Cottage in East Cliff, Dover"
(This image is reproduced in colour in the centre pages).

Prior's interior view of the East Cliff cave-cottage looks towards the open door. The window on the left with its deep sill is clearly cut into the chalk. The window by the door is inserted into a wooden frame that reduces the aperture of the cave entrance. Between the windows is a tall fireplace with mantle, hearth and even the traditional fireside rug.

Furnishings are simple: a high-backed chair, stool and beneath the far window a bench. Plates, cups and bottles are displayed on a 'dresser' that is cut from the chalk, as is the half-room-divider that appears to have its own miniature cave cut into it, presumably for storage purposes. Could the objects on its top be a fossil or shell collection displayed as decoration? Certainly there are other decorative items in the room: the wall immediately above the fireplace has three framed pictures, two square and one ovoid, and in two recesses cut into the chalk at head height are objects that look like ornaments. A mirror is suspended on the pillar of the arch. The woven basket, right foreground, is a typical mawn or fish basket. A full-size spade is propped against the exterior wall.

The cave-cottage had advantages over a traditionally constructed home. The cave's internal temperature would have been fairly uniform throughout the year, keeping the occupants cool in summer and warm in winter. It also offered convenience: a new room could be cut, or a new shelf carved, at no expense other than the effort of labour.

Image 15: Oil Painting by G.C. Newton
(This image is reproduced again in the centre pages).

The benefits of cave-living, mentioned above, were offset by the proximity of the eroding sea. The coastal erosion that led to the dwelling's demise is recorded in the 1871 Census: *'...Houses under the cliff towards the Zig Zag washed away by the sea.'*

The danger of navigating the eroding paths is recorded in the Dover Express of June 1871: *'...a small piece of road had given way causing Widow Ann Claw to fall some 65 feet to her death on the beach from an unfenced path leading to the cave where she had lived for 12 years.'*

The oil painting by G. C. Newton, dating from the last decade of the 19th century, depicts the type of storm that would have eroded the path-ways and ultimately 'washed away' the cliff dwellings.

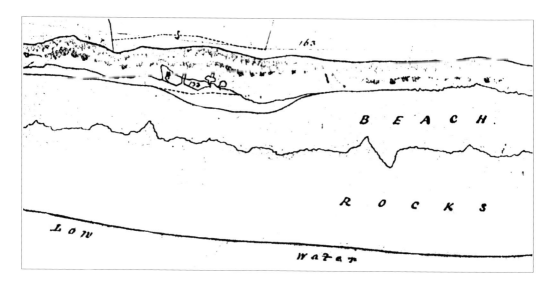

Image 16: Detail from the Tithe map of Guston 1843

Evidence for cave dwellers can be found in the Tithe Map of Guston that shows Mary Burville's property in the cliff-face. From the map it looks as though the entrances of a complex of three caves were on the top of a large cliff fall, below Northfall Meadow, on the western side of Langdon Cliff. This would place the caves in the middle of the present Eastern Docks, to the east of the Jubilee Way flyover.

The map is complemented by the Tithe Return of 1843 which lists landowners and occupiers and records that Mary Burville occupied a Cottage in the Cliff together with 13 perch of land (about 400 sq. yards). The Tithe Return makes no mention of occupants in other caves, but this does not rule out other troglodytes being present at this time.

Part five:
Below Langdon Cliff

Though remote, in the early 19th century, the foreshore beneath Langdon Cliff was a busy location for earning a living, both legitimately and otherwise.

Image 17: "Dover Cliffs from the East" by Thomas Hastings

This 1830 sketch shows a wide cliff-fall with a well-used path tracking over it. The formation of the surrounding cliffs confirms this to be the fall at the base of Langdon Cliff, the location of the Guston cave cottage painted by Prior (see Image 13). The sketch was made before any serious erosion of the cave-cottage fall took place.

The Hastings' sketch shows a figure walking the fall-track. In the middle distance is the East Cliff path and Castle Jetty. Above are some ramparts of Dover Castle, and peeping above these defences is what could be the church tower of St Mary's in Castro. By 1830 the building behind the jetty must be East Cliff Lodge, the villa that replaced Smith's Folly. In the distance is the harbour with the tall masts of many ships and, above them, the familiar shape of Shakespeare Cliff.

The track in this sketch leads to the 'curious road' referred to in the 1830 Dover Guide, by Z Warren of Snargate Street:

> *'Passing from this villa,* (East Cliff Lodge) *and continuing about a mile along the base of the cliff, there is a curious road, ascending from the beach to a watch house on the cliff, (a perpendicular height of upwards of three hundred feet.) This work was executed by government for the accommodation of the officers and men employed in the blockade service There is also a telegraph on the new principle.'*

The 'curious road' is presumably a reference to the zigzag at Langdon Bay, as this led to the watch house and signalling station on the cliff-top.

The pier, Shakespeare's cliff, and (Western) Heights are indicated in the key at the foot of the sketch.

Image 18: "Coast Guard Station, Dover" by W.H. Prior
(This image is reproduced in colour in the centre pages).

At first glance, this watercolour, painted sometime during the period 1833 -1857, is something of a mystery. It depicts a rising full moon illuminating little more than a large rock formation in the foreground and three human figures, two attend a boat drawn up onto the beach, the third stands as if on look-out on a rock at the base of the cliff. An explanation for the caption is that the coast-guard cutters operated from this stretch of shore.

The Coastguard Signalling Station was located on the cliff top above Langdon Bay, where access to the shore was by way of the Langdon Stairs zigzag. An unpublished account by the late S.J.G. Burville, which is supported by Image 20, describes how the Langdon caves were used as boathouses for the coastguard cutters. The two-masted boat is probably a cutter and the figures likely to be men of the counter-smuggling Coastal Prevention Service.

Dover Castle circa 1810 (Image 4)

"East Cliff Cave-Cottage" (Image 13)

"*Cave-Cottage in East Cliff, Dover*" (Image 14)

Oil Painting by G.C. Newton (Image 15)

"Coast Guard Station, Dover" (Image 18)

Uniform of the Preventive Service Blockade by William Heath (Image 19)

Watercolour captioned "Near Dover August 30th 1847 A. P." (Image 20)

Aerial View of the Eastern Docks (Image 41)

Image 19: Uniform of the Preventive Service Blockade by William Heath
(This image is reproduced in colour in the centre pages).

This coloured aquatint, dated 1822, depicts a man of the Preventive Service Blockade. He is armed with a brace of pistols and a sword, the latter suggesting he holds officer rank. The location must be Langdon Bay, where the Langdon Stairs zigzag connected the shore with the cliff-top Blockade or Coastguard station. The unusual rock that dominates the portrait is almost certainly that depicted in the previous watercolour by Prior.

There is no safe mooring at this spot and the capstan behind the central figure would have been used to pull Preventive Service Cutters above the high-tide mark and into the shelter of caves.

Image 20: Watercolour captioned "Near Dover August 30th 1847 A. P."
(This image is reproduced in colour in the centre pages).

The artist views the Dover Straits from the interior of a large cave, which is functioning as a boathouse.

The slim bow of the boat suggests the racing lines of a coastguard cutter. The man at the cave-mouth wears clothes not dissimilar to those of the Blockade officer above. Though the barrels evident on the left of the cave suggest the romance of smuggling activity, it is far more likely that this cave is that at Langdon Bay which was used by the Preventive Service who countered such illegal activities.

Part six:
Caves, Tracks and People

The constant erosion of the cliff-face and the various attempts to counteract the forces of nature can be studied in the following sequence of photographs.

Image 21: 1850 photograph of the low-tide eastern cliffs

At first glance, this 1850 photograph appears unremarkable, except for the grandeur of the cliffs. However, computer-enhancement reveals its secrets as seen in Images 21a -21h. To take this view, the photographer must have been standing near the spot where the carrier is shown in Image 11.

In the foreground are cart tracks and a collection of large flints that have been raised from the foreshore. Though the chalk road appears to end, vestiges of its continuation can be traced as paths over the tops of distant, eroded falls.

Image 21a: The Carrier

On the chalk road is a horse, with one wheel of its cart clearly visible. To the rear of the cart are the back legs and tail of a second horse that is being attended by the carrier, a very satisfying confirmation of the horse-drawn vehicle depicted in earlier engravings.

The horse and cart at this precise spot is explained by the presence of caves used by the carriers for storage. The short flight of chalk-cut steps behind the horse gave access to one of these caves. Its entrance can be seen in the bare piece of projecting smooth chalk immediately above the steps.

A few yards beyond these steps is the beginning of a path leading to higher caves whose entrances are hidden by the jutting cliff. Fencing erected in front of one of the caves can be seen some 25 feet above the horse. In 1870 this path was later extended into a track that led to an excavated tunnel providing access to the cliff-top.

Image 21b: Money for Old Stones

Beyond the steps and horses, several irregularly shaped piles can be seen. Under magnification, these piles are clearly of shingle. Presumably the flints are destined for transportation by carrier's cart, as wheel tracks are clearly visible in the chalk road (see Image 21). In 1812 the Dover Paving Commission paid two shillings (10p) for a ton weight cartload of gravel and one shilling & two pence (6p) for the same weight of stones. By 1870, shingle was being supplied at three shillings and seven pence (17p) a cubic yard.

In front of these shingle piles and overhanging the shore, is a platform complete with winch. The winching point would have been used to raise flints, seaweed or cargo, from the beach. Beneath the winch platform is a handrail suggesting a route leading either down to the beach or to the lower level twin caves, seen in close-up in Image 27a.

Image 21c: Broadlees Bottom

A line of fencing is visible at Broadlees Bottom. At the cliff-edge section is a well-trodden pathway. This raises an interesting question, how did the cliff-top walkers descend to the road level at East Cliff before the construction of the 1870 tunnel? It seems unlikely that they went through or round the castle to Dover! Perhaps the ladder partly visible in Image 25a provides the answer.

Image 21d: Fox Hill Down

On the distant cliff top of Fox Hill Down, above Langdon Cliff, the change of shading is evidence of agricultural activity.

Image 21e: The Caves

At the foot of Langdon Cliff, (middle-ground) further steps, relatively unworn and possibly recently cut or renewed, connect the path on the vestigial fall with the shore. The beach steps and related path lead directly to the black shape of a cave entrance. To the left of this opening is another framed entrance. Computer image-enhancement reveals a door, window, low chalk walls and the suggestion of a chimneystack (see image overleaf). This layout is almost identical to the external view of the East Cliff Cave Cottage as painted by W.H. Prior.

Image 21f: Dover's Troglodytes

Remarkably, this early photograph appears to have captured two of Dover's troglodytes. In the computer enhancement two figures, a male and female, appear to be chatting over the wall outside the cave entrance.

Image 21g: Tax Avoidance?

On the shingle, directly in front of the steps leading to the caves, is a pile of material with the shaft of a shovel clearly visible. The regular mound shape of this pile suggests that it is coal off-loaded from a boat. Whilst this may have been the usual way to deliver fuel to the inhabitants of the Guston caves, another possibility is that it was intended for transportation, by carrier's cart, rather further afield in order to avoid the levy that would be incurred by landing at Dover. At this time the Dover Pavement Commission was levying a charge of 12% on materials, such as coal, coke, culm (coal dust), cinders, ashes and charcoal brought into the town and port of Dover.

Image 21h: Beach People

To the east of this pile are three figures, one of whom is sitting on the beach and could be sketching. At the foot of the cliff, above and to the right of these figures, the stern of a boat, possibly a coastguard cutter, can be seen pulled up above the high water mark.

Image 22: Undated Photograph of the Eastern Cliffs

The piles of shingle, winch and fencing patterns look much the same as those recorded in the previous 1850 photograph. However, evidence of agricultural activity on the cliff-top fields suggests a date some years later for this Image.

Though both background and foreground are in focus, one feature, the winch, is blurred. The blurring suggests that the winch was in use when the photograph was being taken. With no winch-man or handle visible, it is likely that the winch was being used as a pulley operated from the beach.

Image 22a: The Winch and Grading of Shingle

The shingle piles on the road are complemented by similar piles on the beach. Footprints and evidence of digging are proof of human activity since the last high tide. A sieving process is a likely explanation for the conical shape of these piles with indentation marks in the beach suggesting a tripod support for such a device. Presumably sieves were used in order to grade the shingle for particular needs.

Image 23: Eastward view from East Cliff Jetty

This undated photograph, taken at high tide, may well be contemporary with Image 21 of 1850 as it shows similar features, such as the configuration of the cliff falls and the same vestiges of cliff track. The central feature of picket fencing is identical to that in front of Athol Terrace in Image 30 and therefore serves to locate this shot. The wooden construction, bottom right, is likely to be connected to the out-of-frame East Cliff Jetty.

Apart from the picket fencing, other new features revealed are: i) two groynes, though the one in the foreground is almost completely hidden by its bank of shingle, and ii) a dilapidated, wooden construction behind the fencing. The scale of the latter is hard to judge. The structure could be a winch-housing or something larger. Two boats, probably Coastguard cutters, are drawn up on the shingle bank at Langdon Bay, where the Coastguard Service used the caves as boathouses.

In the foreground, above the sea defence, is a pile of flints reminiscent of those in other photographs in this set. Above Broadlees Bottom, top left, there is a gap in the fencing where it crosses the footpath. At this point a tall post has been added, its purpose far from obvious.

Image 24: Undated Cliff study by Jacolette, Dover.

This view, attributed to Martin Jacolette, shows a section of cliff at low tide. By its scouring action, the sea has removed the shingle to reveal the underlying chalk bedrock, scattered with large rocks.

Evidence of cliff-falls, long eroded, can be seen in the striations cut into the bedrock by the powerful force of the sliding chalk. Interestingly, the erosion of the most distant cliff-fall would suggest that this photograph is directly contemporary with the following 1870 Image. As Jacolette was a photographer in the area from 1887 to 1909, he may have been working from an earlier plate by another photographer.

Along the tops of the undulating and eroded cliff-falls, vestiges of the old track still survive. Associated with the nearest piece of path are some rudimentary steps. Presumably these were cut to replace steps further to the west that had been buried by a cliff-fall.

The shading on the cliff-top at Fox Hill Down is evidence of agricultural activity.

Image 25: Cliffs Viewed from the Eastern End of Athol Terrace, 1870

To capture this view, the photographer must have been standing at a point almost level with the East Cliff chalk road.

The agricultural activity, noted on Fox Hill Down in previous images, has been extended towards the cliff edge. At the cliff top of Broadlees Bottom a secondary line of fencing has appeared. This takes the form of two white solid, gate-type constructions. Nearby is what appears to be some sort of large notice board. Minutes from a meeting of the Dover Chamber of Commerce, September 1870, record:

> 'The question of the fence erected upon land of the Earl of Guilford across the footpath leading to St Margaret's, and the notice placed there, warning the public from trespassing, was entered upon; and the Secretary was directed to write to the Earl, stating that the Chamber is confident that his lordship would not willingly do anything to obstruct the wants of the public, and that the Chamber is at the same time anxious to prevent damage to the property, and proposing to substitute for the present another notice, warning the public from trespassing on the land at the side of the footpath along the cliff.'

Beneath the Earl's notice board, the sun shines on some recently exposed chalk where a person can just be discerned. This disturbance of chalk is the result of Borough Surveyor John Hanvey's explosion that created a tunnel to give new access to the cliff top. What looks like a newly excavated path, leading up from the chalk road, is in fact a widening of an existing track to give improved access to the tunnel entrance.

The winch evident in earlier photographs has disappeared, as have the associated piles of flint, but the steps leading up from the chalk road are still visible. On the shore, the shingle has been scoured out by gales, leaving an inhospitable, rocky littoral.

Image 25a: Scaling the Cliff

The flotsam and jetsam fencing, in front of the cave above the steps, is a survival from 1850. At the left-hand end of this cave site is a ladder, which may have been used to reach gulls' nests for the purpose of egg collection and, possibly, to enable people to scale the cliff prior to the 1870 tunnel being constructed.

A woman and two more shadowy figures appear on the chalk road, just below the ladder. The shadow could represent a single man either unaware of, or too impatient to stand still for, the photographer.

Image 26: Ink and Wash Drawing by Henry Wyndham, 1869.

This dramatic view, drawn almost two decades after some of the early photographic evidence, shows the extent of the East Cliff track. Presumably artistic licence was employed to recreate the track and its travellers as it might have appeared rather earlier in the century. One traveller is waving a staff, the other has one sloped over his shoulder in military fashion.

From the configuration of the cliffs, the piece of track travelled by the human figures is on the section of cliff directly beneath the Jubilee Way over-pass that carries the A2 road into the Eastern Docks.

The sketch seems to have been made from a point just east of the flint pile captured in the 1850 photograph, (see Image 21). If this location is accurate, then the boarded steps featured in the drawing would be those behind the carrier's horse and cart, seen in close-up in Image 21a.

Wyndham has dramatised the low-tide shore by strewing it with boulders, a rocky appearance often produced by the scouring action of the sea.

Image 27:View from Athol Terrace, 1875

This is one of several 19th century photographs taken from the eastern end of Athol Terrace. The date attribution of 1875 would seem to be accurate as the 1877 sea-defence concrete bulwark below the twin caves has not yet been built though Hanvey's tunnel is much in evidence.

The photograph is signed E.V. Bowles, Dover. As Bowles was operating as photographer from 1909-1931 he must have been working from an earlier plate.

In the centre of this photograph, beneath Langdon Cliff, a major cliff fall can be seen extending out to sea. The fall must have been recent as the chalk above tide-level is white and devoid of vegetation. West of this fall, part-way up the cliff, is all that remains of the East Cliff cave-cottage. Erosion has exposed the cave's interior giving it the appearance of a black hole. Another chalk-slide on the St Margaret's side of the cliff-top fencing has obliterated the steps connecting the caves with the shore. These steps were clearly visible in the photographic littoral-scape of 1850.

On the left of the photograph, the rectangular doorway located halfway up the cliff is another cave cottage (seen more clearly overleaf). Its entrance appears to have square-cut windows to each side. Access to this dwelling was probably by way of the steps visible in Image 21a.

Image 27a: The Twin Caves

This close-up reveals two caves just below the unfenced chalk road. A well-worn path leads down to them. These caves are situated in the lower cliff, beyond the foreground sea-defences. Though near to Athol Terrace, their vulnerability to high tides makes it unlikely that they were used for habitation. The worn condition of the path suggests a regular usage, presumably for storage purposes.

Image 28: Guston Cliff with Sea Defence and Track

This image probably dates from 1891 as a similar photograph of that date can be found in the Frith postcard collection. The track above the lower twin caves is now fenced for the whole of its length. This fencing was installed after the excavation, in 1870, of the Hanvey tunnel that gave access to the cliff top.

Several new features appear in this last decade of the 19th century:

i)   the stone bastion-style defence below the lower level twin caves, part of the sea defence work undertaken in 1877.

ii)   the massive target, anchored by wire stays and wooden struts, erected on the cliff-top military rifle range, near the Earl of Guilford's white notice board. "A Plan of the Volunteer Review at Dover", dated March 29th 1869, shows a rifle range and butts located in this part of Broadlees Bottom. The rifle range does not appear on a plan of two years earlier.

iii)   on the seaward side of the cliff-top path is a sentry-box construction with an occupant. This is likely to be a shelter for the target monitor, connected with the rifle range.

iv)   at the peak of Fox Hill Down is a tall mast flying a flag to warn that the firing range was operational.

v)   the cliff-top path, nearest the castle, is now fenced on both the sea and landslides. The fencing would have guided walkers to the entrance of the tunnel, avoiding trespass on the Earl of Guilford's land.

vi)   the corner of walling visible at Langdon Hole is the boundary of the Langdon Convict Prison.

vii) the well-worn footpaths, taking an inland route to the top of Fox Hill Down, suggest a shift in destination-interest from earlier photographs. At least one of these paths would have connected with the track to the Langdon Convict Prison.

viii) the purpose of the line of three posts on the shore is unknown but was likely used in earlier sea-defence work.

In the right foreground is the figure of a boy with a white collar. Perhaps the objects he carries are the spoils of hovelling (a local term that embraced beach-combing as well as opportunist boating-activity). A further figure, facing the photographer, leans on the fencing immediately below the tunnel entrance.

The cave-like opening at the end of the fenced track is the entrance to the tunnel referred to by C.T. Paske in his book "Sunny Dover", dated 1894, as:

'...a short cut, through a tunnel, up to the back of the Castle and the grassy downs. The conception of this outlet, which I cannot remember having seen during either of my earlier visits, was a happy idea and its execution a great boon, shortening as it does the road to Deal via St Margaret's over the downs.'

An 1876 Dover Guide attributes the building of the tunnel to a Dover Chamber of Commerce initiative under the supervision of John Hanvey, who was Borough Surveyor from August 1861 until November 1879. Dover Express newspaper archives reveal that the

Image 28a: Hanvey's Tunnel

tunnel was excavated in 1870. Above and to the right of the tunnel entrance is a dark rectangular cut. In an unpublished account, the late S.J.G. Burville writes: *'But a hole to give light was made half-way along the tunnel & I well remember, as a child, being lifted up to see the ships through the hole in the tunnel.'* His account would seem to be confirmed by a report in the Dover Express stating that a gallery was being constructed from the tunnel to the face of the cliff. The rectangular cut evident in this photograph is undoubtedly this window or gallery. Photographic evidence of the cliff-top entrance to this tunnel can be seen in Image 33a.

In September 1870, the Dover Express recorded the appointment of a man named Oliver to take charge of the tunnel at an allowance of 2/6d (12.5p) a week. Oliver's duties included sweeping the tunnel path and preventing the disorderly proceedings of *'...boys rushing in at the top of the tunnel and howling at the top of their voices while wayfarers were ascending.'*

Image 29: Langdon Convict Prison, taken from an aerial reconnaissance photograph

The prison was created to accommodate convicts, envisaged as labour for the building of the National Harbour. However, objections were raised and the convict labour was never employed for this purpose. According to a report in the Dover Express, the prison had been used for those undergoing their first sentence of Penal Servitude and prisoners were engaged in *'sewing mail bags and other light employment.'*

Construction of the prison began in 1884 with locally-made bricks brought by horse tramway from the Dover-Deal road. The first convicts were installed in August 1885 and the prison was in civil use from then until the mid-1890s. (The O.S. 25 map of 1896 bears the legend "Her Majesty's Prison Disused"). From 1901 until 1908 it was used as a military prison, and as a barracks during the First World War. Demolition of the prison, by this time more usually known as Langdon Barracks, began in 1924, though the walls were still standing in 1939. The site was finally cleared in the 1950s. An 1889 plan of the prison, shows its three-terrace construction. These terraces survive today as the parking and viewing areas at the National Trust and Saga's Gateway to the White Cliffs' Visitor Centre at Langdon Cliffs.

Part seven:
Castle Jetty and Athol Terrace

The jetty, groynes and other sea-defences enabled people to inhabit a previously remote and inhospitable area of the coast.

Image 30: Athol Terrace, circa 1865

This photograph returns us to Castle Jetty, where the photographer George Thomas Amos, of 70 Biggin Street, has parked his mobile studio. At this date, Number 15 Athol Terrace, the property on the extreme right, is a two-story building. Later it was to be rebuilt with a third floor.

At various dates in the 19th century different areas in front of the houses were enclosed by picket fencing on a collective, rather than individual house, basis. At this time, there is a tall flagpole at a corner of the fencing.

A passage-way, between numbers 8 and 9 Athol Terrace, leads to eight small cottages known as Athol Court (though sometimes referred to as Athol Cottages). The entrance passage to these dwellings, part obscured by a sloping wall, can be seen above and to the right of the top-hatted man on the jetty. Chimneys, roofs and walls of these cottages can be seen in Image 33b. The stepped sea defences are identical to those shown on the O.S. Map of Castle Ward dated 1859.

Image 31: 19th Century Athol Terrace, taken from the Jetty

This view of Athol Terrace bathed in early morning sunlight is variously dated as 1865 and 1868, but both attributions are probably too early.

The sea defences look in good order and are no longer stepped. This suggests that the photograph was taken after sea defence work was carried out in 1877. Under the East Cliff Sea Defences Act, owners of adjoining properties were specially rated to fund the work carried out by Dover Town Council. Benjamin and William Burville, previously of the cave-cottage and now living at numbers 45 and 47 East Cliff, are recorded as paying these special rates. The now defunct groynes are in a ruinous condition.

The picket-fenced area at the front of the terrace is now restricted to the four houses at the eastern end and the undercliff chalk road is unfenced.

The position of the two groynes, in relation to Athol Terrace, helps to precisely locate several features identified in the other eastward-looking views in this set of photographs.

Image 31a: Entrance to Athol Court

To the left of the two-wheeled coal-loaded cart, is the dark entrance of a passage-way leading to the cottages of Athol Court.

Image 32: "Site of Proposed Undercliff Drive, Dover"

This image, circa 1895, is taken from the jetty end of Athol Terrace. At this date, the sea defences in front of Athol Terrace are triple-stepped.

The concept of an undercliff drive was stimulated by the proposal to build the Admiralty Harbour. It would have extended the chalk road that already existed beyond East Cliff, the fencing of which is clearly visible in the middle ground of this photograph.

The purpose of the drive was to give access to the South Foreland in order to open it up for residential development. A similar scheme had been mooted in 1844 following the arrival of the railway. In that year, the Earl of Guilford proposed a development to the north of the castle, comprising about 1500 houses arranged in grand terraces, with an approach road from Castle Jetty. Fortunately for the natural character of Dover's famous white cliffs neither scheme was carried out.

The large rifle-range target and the nearby Earl of Guilford's white notice board are still evident on the cliff-top.

Part eight:
Dover Bay and the Harbour

In the last decades of the 19th and early decades of the 20th century, building projects transformed Dover Bay. The greatest of these was the construction of the Admiralty or National Harbour. Other additions were the Promenade Pier and the Prince of Wales Pier. The Admiralty harbour was originally handed over to the Dover Harbour Board for civil use in 1923. During World War Two, the harbour was again occupied by the navy but was transferred back to the Harbour Board in September 1945. At the end of hostilities, cross-channel traffic boomed and car-ferry berths were constructed in the Eastern Dock to handle this traffic. The expansion of the docks continued throughout the last century.

Image 33: East Cliff, viewed from the Cliffs

The wide aspect of this westward-looking, low-tide cliffscape includes East Cliff, Dover sea front and Shakespeare Cliff. The photograph was probably taken from the cliff-edge in the vicinity of the target featured in Image 28. A central point of interest in this photograph is the Promenade Pier. Building of the pier commenced in December 1891. The pier proved so popular that, in 1901, a pavilion was constructed at its end to be used for orchestral concerts and other entertainment. By 1913 the pier was being used as an Admiralty landing jetty, but by 1927 it became unsafe, and was demolished.

Beyond the Promenade Pier the commencement of the Prince of Wales Pier can be seen as an iron viaduct entering the sea from the beach. This work was begun in 1893, thus dating this photograph precisely.

Paths provide access to the upper and lower entrances to Hanvey's tunnel linking Athol Terrace with the cliff-top. The two groynes this side of the jetty are in disrepair and appear as stumps projecting from the beach.

On the shore, several groups of people can be seen while two more walk the fenced, chalk road. At the beachhead, beyond Castle Jetty, are several capstans and numerous boats pulled up on the shingle beach.

Image 33a: Cliff-top Tunnel Entrance

On the extreme right, the beginning of a sloping handrail provides rare evidence of the cliff-top entrance to John Hanvey's tunnel. The tunnel was of sufficient importance to be mentioned in the renowned Baedeker "Great Britain Handbook", of 1890, where it states that the tunnel '...*is closed when rifle-shooting is being practised in the North Fall Meadow*'.

Image 33b: Athol Court

At the rear of Athol Terrace, and at right angles to it, are the two rows of the eight small cottages of Athol Court. These dwellings had a cellar, living-room, washroom, yard and privy, and a 1st & 2nd floor bedroom. They were built in two rows at right angle to the rear of Athol Terrace, feature in various records including an East Cliff plan of 1861 and Census returns of 1851, 1871 and 1891. The latter census records only six of the eight properties as being occupied. The court fell into disuse for human habitation between 1901 and 1905, probably because of the threat of falling chalk, although six Athol Court properties appear on the Ordnance Survey town map of 1907. The entrance to these cottages can be seen in Images 30 and 31a.

It is difficult to believe that this community of eight households existed in what are now the back-gardens of two or three of the houses in Athol Terrace. Walls, of one of the two rows of cottages, are still very much in evidence.

The white triangle next to the cliff-top fencing is a marker connected with the military rifle range.

Image 33c: Military Activity

Image 34: East Cliff from the East, Showing Jetty, Path and Caves

Another cliffscape looking towards East Cliff this time taken at high tide from the track, west of Mary Burville's cave. The centre of focus is the two dark shadows, high on the cliff. These are possibly cave entrances that are not visible in any of the eastward-looking illustrations.

The track in the foreground is a continuation of the higher path that branches from the fenced, East Cliff pathway.

Image 35: View from Cobbler Point

A photograph taken from The Cobbler, also known as Cobbler Point. The stones on each side of the well-worn path would seem to mark the boundary between the parishes of Guston and St Margaret's at Cliffe. But why the duplication of stones, and why should the more recent-looking be located in the more vulnerable, cliff-edge position?

The distant Promenade Pier again appears without its later pavilion. As there is also no sign of the Prince of Wales Pier, this photograph must date from before the commencement of its construction in 1893. Castle Jetty and the smaller jetty below Mote's Bulwark are prominent, as are the coastal defences at Athol Terrace. The track running along the fall-tops is visible, as is a fall-top cave, which is almost certainly one of the caves seen in close-up in the previous image. The large cliff-fall, in the middle ground, is at Langdon Bay.

Below the skyline and Dover Castle is a line of cannons left over from the Napoleonic defences. The tall mast on Fox Hill Down is likely to be a flagpole for warning when the military were firing on the rifle range. To the right of the mast, at the high point of the down, is a dark bank which might be the site of a platform for cannons as shown on the 1869 "Plan of the Volunteer Review at Dover". To the right of this bank is a chalk scar, probably the track leading to the Langdon Convict Prison.

Image 36: East Cliff Sea Defences

This photograph was taken in the last decade of the 19th century when the large target on the military rifle range had been removed. However, the flagpole associated with the range remains on the crest of Fox Hill Down.

Careful examination reveals a number of walkers, particularly on the shore. A likely explanation for the presence of so many people is that the photograph was taken just prior to 1898 when work started on the Admiralty Harbour and the massive extent of cliff excavation would have rendered this area out-of-bounds. On the shore, there are three separate groups walking on the rocks, whilst a woman, in a hat, is seated on a boulder between the bastion-style sea defences.

Image 36a: Cliff-bottom Tunnel Entrance

This close-up shows the lower twin caves and above them the entrance to the Hanvey tunnel. A standing figure appears on the outside of the fencing near the tunnel entrance, and a further person is silhouetted against the white chalk, beneath the notice board, by the upper entrance to the tunnel.

Image 37: The Facing of Langdon Cliff, circa 1898

This eastward looking view, c. 1898, shows the railway track and work in progress on the facing of the cliff, preliminary to the construction of the Admiralty Harbour. The photograph is taken from a similar position to the earlier Image 28.

In comparing these two views, the extent of the facing work is obvious. A huge volume of the mighty cliff-head of Fox Hill Down has been excavated away. The route over the falls that once led to the caves and Langdon Stairs' zigzag, has been obliterated by thousands of tons of chalk, and with it all trace of Hanvey's tunnel and the troglodyte caves. Still preserved in this photograph is the end of the chalk road, the upper two-window cave and the steps leading down to the lower-level twin caves. All these features were soon to disappear as the cliff facing advanced towards East Cliff.

The notice board on the beach states:

ADMIRALTY HARBOUR & WORKS

IT IS DANGEROUS

TO PASS ALONG THE SHORE BETWEEN

THIS BOARD AND LANGDON BAY.

Presumably a similar warning was posted on the board erected on the chalk-road above.

The present-day path leading from Athol Terrace to the Langdon Cliff top can be seen in Image 38.

Image 37a: Work in Progress

Against the vastness of the chalk scar, workers engaged in the facing of the cliff appear as lines of black ants.

Image 38: Construction of the Admiralty Harbour

In this photograph, the cliff facing associated with the building of the Harbour has progressed towards Athol Terrace. Rolling stock for conveying the chalk can be seen on the lower railway-lines, whilst a steam engine moves on the upper rails. The upper railway is cut into the old chalk road that ran from Athol Terrace and a new higher-level fenced way, complete with telegraph poles, has been created. The new path is obviously popular with walkers.

The cusp in the faced cliffs is located at Broadlees Bottom where the present day Jubilee Way extends the A2 road into the Eastern Docks. On the far side of this cusp is the terrace of coastguard houses surviving to the present day. The other buildings, apparently located on the castle-side of the cusp, are long gone.

Image 38a: The Carrier's Cave

The vegetation-topped lump of chalk behind the open wagons, and the area immediately beneath the figures leaning on the fence above, are the remaining remnants of the original cliff-face. From the alignment of these original features, it seems likely that the cave below the fencing is one of those used by the carriers and accessed from the original chalk road (see Image 21a).

Image 39: Construction of Car-Ferry Berths

Taken from Langdon Cliff, this 1953 photograph shows the construction of the original car-ferry berths at the Eastern Docks.

Image 40: Ferry Berths in Operation

The car-ferry berths in operation, photographed a decade after their inauguration in June 1953.

In the background are the pens built for Motor Torpedo Boats and later used for submarines. These pens were swallowed up in subsequent land reclamation for dock expansion some three decades later.

A third berth was added in 1966 to meet increased demand and the threat of the proposed Channel Tunnel. Major redevelopment of the car-ferry terminal was carried out in 1968-1970. Expansion continued, and in the 1970s further land was reclaimed from the sea to provide a new double-decker ferry berth and freight assembly space. A fifth berth opened in 1975.

Image 41: Aerial View of the Eastern Docks
(This image is reproduced in colour in the centre pages).

This end-of-millennium aerial view shows the extensive development at the Eastern Docks, and the Jubilee Way viaduct that opened in July 1977.

The properties that comprise Athol Terrace and the most distant cliffs towards the South Foreland appear little changed from previous centuries. However, nothing remains of Cobbler Point, the track over the falls, the troglodyte caves, or the Hanvey tunnel. All these features were obliterated during the building of the Admiralty Harbour at the end of the 19th century.

The final decade of the 20th century saw extensive reclamation of the sea area inside the enclosed harbour. Sand dredged from the Goodwins was used as a base for road widening and lorry-parking facilities. This infilling swallowed much of Castle Jetty and the beach to the west of it. The Jetty, once a magnet for promenaders, was reduced to little more than a pencil stub, while the loss of beach resulted in the disappearance of the small boats that had, for so long, been the means of livelihood for many of East Cliff's residents.

General Index ~ Image Number

Index of Artists and Photographers ~ Image Number